MACDONALD STARTERS

Cats

Macdonald Educational

About Macdonald Starters

Macdonald Starters are vocabulary controlled information books for young children. More than ninety per cent of the words in the text will be in the reading vocabulary of the vast majority of young readers. Word and sentence length have also been carefully controlled.

Key new words associated with the topic of each book are repeated with picture explanations in the Starters dictionary at the end. The dictionary can also be used as an index for teaching children to look things up.

Teachers and experts have been consulted on the content and accuracy of the books.

Illustrated by: Esme Eve

Editors: Peter Usborne, Su Swallow, Jennifer Vaughan

Reading consultant: Donald Moyle, author of *The Teaching of Reading* and senior lecturer in education at Edge Hill College of Education

Chairman, teacher advisory panel: F. F. Blackwell, general inspector for schools, London Borough of Croydon, with responsibility for primary education

Teacher panel: Elizabeth Wray, Loveday Harmer, Lynda Snowdon, Joy West

ⓒ Macdonald and Company (Publishers) 1971
Second Impression 1973
Made and printed in Great Britain by Purnell & Sons Limited Paulton, Somerset

First published 1971 by Macdonald and Company (Publishers) Limited St Giles House 49-50 Poland Street London W1

All these cats live in our street.

This is my cat.
She is looking for food.
She has found some meat to eat.

2

Now she is washing herself.
She licks her paws.
She rubs her ears and whiskers.
with her wet paws.

These cats are male cats.
They are called tomcats.
Tomcats often fight.
4

A big dog comes along.
The cats are afraid.
They all run away.

This cat is climbing a tree.
Cats can climb quickly.
6

The cat is angry.
He is spitting.
The cat's fur is standing up.

Cats like to be alone.
This cat is hunting at night.

8

Cats' eyes are not like ours.
They have special eyes.
They can see well at night.

9

This cat has seen a mouse.
She waits.
Then she jumps on the mouse.
She catches it in her claws.
10

Cats must keep
their claws sharp.
They need sharp claws for hunting.
This cat is sharpening her claws.

Most farmers keep cats.
The cats live in the barns.
They hunt rats and mice.

12

Sailors once kept cats.
They kept cats on ships.
Lots of rats lived on the ships.
The cats hunted the rats.

13

These people lived long ago.
They are Egyptians.
They loved cats.

The Egyptians made statues of cats.

15

The Romans kept cats too.
They went to many countries.
They took their cats with them.
16

Birman

Burmese

Siamese

Russian Blue

Here are some cats
from other countries.

17

All baby cats are called kittens.
18

Kittens love to play.
They play at hunting and fighting.

This cat was lost.
He must hunt for his food.
He has turned wild.

Once all cats were wild.
Then people fed them.
So the cats stayed
with the people.

There are lots of stories
about witches.
The witches kept black cats.

22

Starter's **Cats** words

street
(page 1)

whiskers
(page 3)

meat
(page 2)

paws
(page 3)

eat
(page 2)

fight
(page 4)

lick
(page 3)

dog
(page 5)

ears
(page 3)

climb
(page 6)

23

tree
(page 6)

spit
(page 7)

fur
(page 7)

hunt
(page 8)

night
(page 8)

eyes
(page 9)

mouse
(page 10)

catch
(page 10)

claws
(page 10)

sharpen
(page 11)

farmer
(page 12)

barn
(page 12)

rat
(page 12)

sailor
(page 13)

ship
(page 13)

Egyptian
(page 14)

statue
(page 15)

Roman
(page 16)

kitten
(page 18)

witch
(page 22)

25